Canadian representatives: General Publishing Co., Ltd., 30 Lesmill Road, Don Mills, Ontario M3B 2T6.
International representatives: Worldwide Media Services, Inc., 115 East Twenty-third Street, New York,
New York 10010.

ISBN 0-89471-805-3
Research by Renée Anderson
Cover design by Toby Schmidt
Interior design by Eric Walker
Cover illustration by Bonnie Timmons
Interior illustrations by Bonnie Timmons
Typography by Commcor Communications Corporation, Philadelphia, Pennsylvania
Printed by Howard Printing

This book may be ordered by mail from the publisher. Please add $2.50 for postage and handling
for each copy. *But try your bookstore first!* Running Press Book Publishers, 125 South Twenty-second
Street, Philadelphia, Pennsylvania 19103

PIG
TALES

Running Press
Philadelphia, Pennsylvania

P ig is a beautiful
word.
   –Jack Denton Scott
   American writer

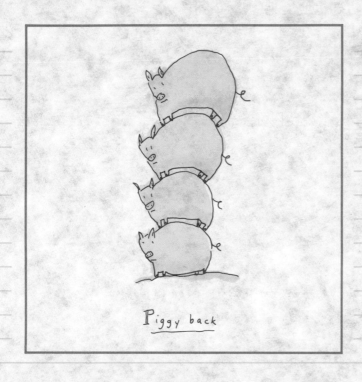

Piggy back

All animals are equal, but some animals are more equal than others.

— *Napoleon, leader of the pigs in* Animal Farm
George Orwell
English writer

The actual lines of a pig (I mean a really fat pig) are among the loveliest and most luxuriant in nature; the pig has the same great curves, swift and yet heavy, which we see in rushing water or in rolling cloud.

—G. K. Chesterton
English journalist
and writer

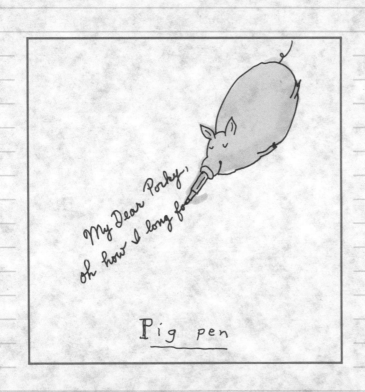

My Dear Porky,
oh how I long fo...

Pig pen

The long, perfect
loveliness of sow.
— *Galway Kinnell*
American poet

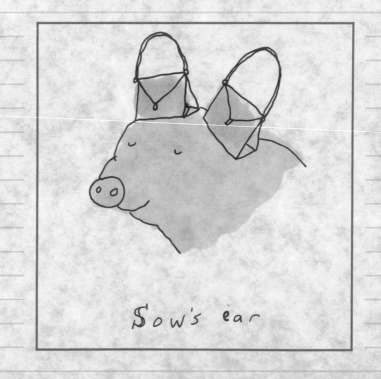

Sow's ear

Whoever has really looked into the eye of a shrewd old sow should feel humility. It is a bright clear eye, more like the eye of a human than the eye of any other animal. It looks at you quite directly, even with what might be called a piercing gaze. The look sizes you up, appraises you.

— Louis Bromfield
American writer

Pig sty

I became purely enamored of her. There were good vibrations. Her eyes are so human too. Like a Kennedy's.

—James Wyeth
American painter
On subject "Dun-Dun"

The love of pigs is an inborn thing. . . . I have always thought that wallowing was a nice quality.

—Sarah Bowman
American writer

Pigs grunt in a wet wallow-bath, and smile as they snort and dream. They dream of the acorned swill of the world, the rooting for pig-fruit, the bag-pipe dugs of the mother sow, the squeal and snuffle of yesses of the women pigs in rut. They mud-bask and snout in the pig-loving sun; their tails curl; they rollick and slobber and snore to deep, smug, after-swill sleep.

— *Dylan Thomas*
Welsh poet

Halloween pig

A pig in almost every cottage sty! That is the infallible mark of a happy people.

−William Cobbett
English journalist
and essayist

Fluellen: What call you the town's name where Alexander the Pig was born?

Gower: Alexander the Great.

Fluellen: Why, I pray you, is not "pig" great? The pig, or the great, or the mighty, or the huge, or the magnanimous, are all one reckonings . . .

—*William Shakespeare*
English playwright
and poet
Henry V, *act IV, scene vii*

Pigmalion

Resting his hands on the rail before him, James Belford swelled before their eyes like a young balloon. The muscles on his cheekbones stood out, his forehead became corrugated, his ears seemed to shimmer. Then, at the very height of the tension, he let it go like, as the poet beautifully puts it, the sound of a great Amen.

"Pig-HOOOOO-OOO-OOO-O-O-ey!"

They looked at him, awed.

— *P. G. Wodehouse*
English writer

A pig does not bolt its food, but chews it, and savors it, and shoves it about with the snout to release the aroma; it revels in it. This, to a pig, is hog heaven.

— Kent Britt
American writer

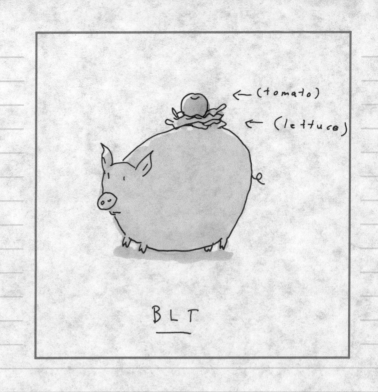

*S*hall I venture to the trough, do I dare to stuff with starches?
I shall dine on low-cal tubers and go on diet marches.
I have heard the farmers talking each to each.
I hope they will not come for me.

—John Southall Hatcher
American writer
and scholar

And there in the wood a Piggy-wig stood,
  With a ring at the end of his nose,
    His nose,
    His nose,
  With a ring at the end of his nose.
  'Dear Pig, are you willing to sell for one shilling
  Your ring?' Said the Piggy, 'I will.'
    — *Edward Lear*
English painter and poet

Ah, a life of adventure is gay and free,

And danger has its charm;

And no pig of spirit will bound his life

By the fence on his master's farm.

—*Walter R. Brooks*
American editor
and writer

Bertie was a pig of action. "Deeds, not grunts," was his motto.

—Kenneth Grahame
Scottish-born
English writer

Greased pig

When the pig de-
cides to snort, well,
everything   will
move.
      – Ian Watters
American sheep farmer

Pigs must have hot blood, they feel like ovens.

—Ted Hughes
English poet

Pigmy

The pig is not especially obstinate; it merely has a tendency to wax hysterical when its equanimity is disturbed.
– *Clifford H. Pope*
American pig expert

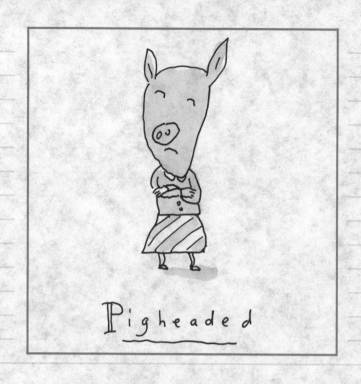

Pigheaded

When Charlotte's web said SOME PIG, Wilbur had tried hard to look like some pig. When Charlotte's web said TERRIFIC, Wilbur had tried to look terrific. And now that the web said RADIANT, he did everything possible to make himself glow.

– E. B. White
American writer

Christmas pig

I never had so much fun in my life as when I was in the field with that pig. He was a smart little rascal and anybody could see he was partial to me. . .
—*Larry Callen*
American writer

There was a young Lady of Bute, who played on a silver-gilt flute;
She played several jigs to her uncle's white pigs,
That amusing Young Lady of Bute.

—Edward Lear
English painter and poet

Swine flu

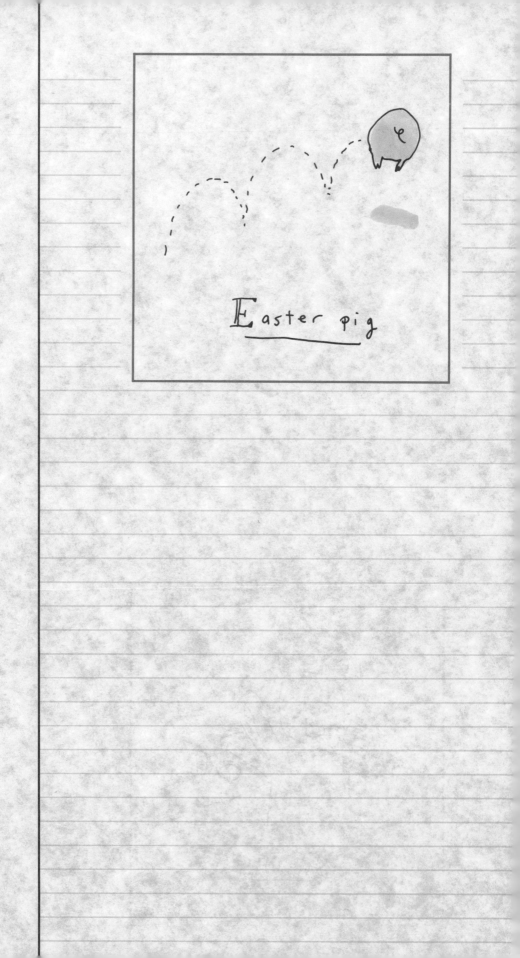

Easter pig

I was brought up
at Hoggenorton
Where pigges play
on the organs.
—*Thomas Nashe*
English playwright

Pigs-in-a-blanket

Nature has played some weird tricks on the pig. It has taken a creature with a brain thought to be inferior only to primates, endowed it with copious amounts of lard, and made it walk on the animal equivalent of high heels.

—Steven Hall
American writer

As anyone knows who has ever had anything to do with pig-keeping, pigs are clever animals. They are not only intelligent, they are extremely adaptable and highly capable of affection for human beings and even of devotion.

—*Edward Hyams*
English writer
and translator

Is there a man among us who on running through a list of his friends is unable to say that there is one among them who is a perfect pig?... I have a friendly feeling toward pigs... I like his disposition and attitude towards all creatures, especially man.... He views us through a totally different, a sort of democratic, standpoint as fellow-citizens and brothers, and takes it for granted, or grunted, that we understand his language, and without servility or insolence he has a natural, pleasant, camerados-all or hail-fellow-well-met air with us.

—*W. H. Hudson*
English naturalist
and writer

Porkypine

I like pigs and I
honestly believe that
most pigs like me.
Hogs are beautiful.
Some of my best
friends are hogs . . . .
But as for me, I like
pigs. Against all who
besmirch them, I
stand ready to speak
in their defense—
even on the floor of
the House of Repre-
sentatives of the U.S.
Congress.

—Fred Schwengel
U. S. Congressman
(R-Iowa)

Perhaps, say some, the hog artfully mirrors the pathos of the country itself: huge, maladroit, and always straining toward some elusive dream beneath yet another clod of dirt.

—*William Hedgepeth*
American writer

Living high on the hog

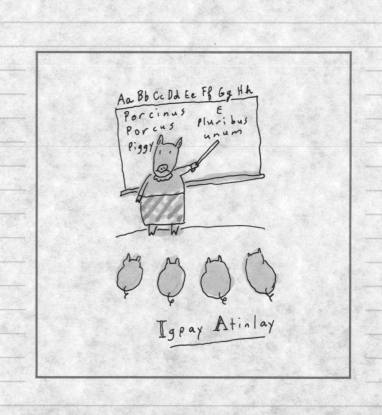

The fact is, compared to pigs, we humans are unforgivably slow to learn from pragmatic experience.

—Karl Schwenke
American writer

In this world,
pigs, as well as
men,
Must dance to for-
tune's fiddlings,
But must I give the
classics up,
For barley-meal and
middlings?
—*Thomas Hood*
English poet

Thanksgiving pig

The last charge
—he lives
A dirty life. Here I
could shelter him
With noble and
right-reverend
precedents,
And show by sanc-
tion of authority
That 'tis a very hon-
orable thing
To thrive by dirty
ways. But let me
rest
On better ground
the unanswerable
defence.
The pig is a philoso-
pher, who knows
No prejudice. Dirt?
Jacob, what is
dirt?"

—Robert Southey
English poet

B ath first," said
Kanga in a cheerful
voice. *"Aha!"* said
Piglet, looking
round anxiously for
the others.

—A. A. Milne
English writer

Pigasus

The time has come,' the Walrus said,
'To talk of many things:
Of shoes—of ships—and sealing wax—
of cabbages—and kings—
And why the sea is boiling hot—
And whether pigs have wings.'

—*Lewis Carroll*
English writer

I have myself a poetical enthusiasm for pigs, and the paradise of my fancy is one where pigs have wings. But it is only men, especially wise men, who discuss whether pigs can fly; we have no particular proof that pigs ever discuss it.

– G. K. Chesterton
English journalist
and writer

I am convinced that pigs too have a fantasy life. Last summer's litter included a little female who thought she was a diva. . . . She projected her fantasy with such piglike conviction that we were forced to acknowledge it. I fully expected to come out of the pen one day and find her on her hind legs, front legs clutched to her full bosoms delivering herself of Brünnhilde's sendoff of Siegfried "Zu neuen Thaten."

—*Karl Schwenke*
American writer

Pig tales

P igs see the
wind.
—*Samuel Butler*
English writer

The white moon, enchanted, turns 'round behind the roofs, and only I, dreamily, remain in the same place. Before me, a transparent pig ecstatically buries its feet in the mud.

—Marc Chagall
Russian painter

Pig pong

The overwhelming conclusion is that pigs are pleasing. The Earth would be poorer in so many ways without them.
—*Jack Denton Scott*
American writer

Piggy bank

Every pig is different..... And I swear they smile at you.

– *Nancy Everman*
Iowa Pork Producer's
Association
Women's Division

I bbity, ibbity, th-
th-that's all folks!
— *Porky Pig*